Summer
WILDCRAFTS

Summer WILDCRAFTS

INSPIRATIONAL PROJECTS HARVESTED FROM NATURE

TESSA EVELEGH

PHOTOGRAPHS BY DEBBIE PATTERSON

LORENZ BOOKS

This edition first published in 1998 by Lorenz Books

© Anness Publishing Limited 1998

Lorenz Books is an imprint of.
Anness Publishing Limited
Hermes House
88–89 Blackfriars Road
London SE1 8HA

This edition published in the USA by Lorenz Books,
Anness Publishing Inc., 27 West 20th Street,
New York, NY 10011; (800) 354-9657

This edition distributed in Canada by
Raincoast Books, 8680 Cambie Street,
Vancouver, British Columbia V6P 6M9

ISBN 1 85967 613 8

A CIP catalogue record for this book is
available from the British Library

Publisher: Joanna Lorenz
Project Editor: Joanne Rippin
Designer: Nigel Partridge
Photographer: Debbie Patterson
Stylist: Tessa Evelegh
Illustrator: Attic Publishing

Printed and bound in Singapore

10 9 8 7 6 5 4 3 2 1

CONTENTS

INTRODUCTION

In most of us, there is a strong desire both to collect and to create, and that is what this book is all about. It is about seeing beauty in the world all around us – a lush green leaf, a delicate feather, a sculpted shell, an extrovert flower – and using it to make beautiful things for the home. There are ideas for using flowers and plants, leaves and blossoms, eggs, feathers and twigs, all of which are icons of spring and summer in themselves. Some of the projects are simply a new twist on a flower display that can be created for a special occasion, or ways to add

ABOVE: A May-time field of delicate, yellow Californian poppies in Oregon, USA.

flair to celebration table settings. Others offer inspiration for home décor and accessories using nature's own favourite materials. There are new ideas here, as well as old ideas based on traditional folk art skills.

The key to wildcrafts is to bear in mind its twofold nature: collecting and creating. The collecting is an important part of the creating, as it very often provides the inspiration for what is to be made. One of the most dramatic examples in this book is the Wild Barley Ring. I had intended to make dandelion orbs, but a hot spell a week before the photographs were taken meant that the dandelions had all gone to seed by the time they were needed. On our next day of photography, however, I found under the trees an abundance of rippling wild barley, soft and feathery, in that unique and delicate sheen of celadon green. What a gift! A huge armful cut with a pocket knife made no mark on the growing display, and the idea for a charming feathery ring was born.

Take children on a walk in the country, and you'll find it almost impossible to stop them picking up beautiful leaves. On the beach, each pebble will appear more desirable than the last.

LEFT: Bluebells and red campion in rainy woodland that is bursting with the vigour of early spring.

ABOVE: An uncommon sight in these days of intensive farming, a beautiful English meadow of daisies and poppies blazes with colour in the summer sunshine.

Whether or not you have children, thinking about making something with natural materials opens your eyes to their beauty, and you can have real enjoyment collecting them. But while everything in this book is inspired by the wild, you don't have to go out into the wilderness to assemble all the materials. Flowers, plants and eggs can be found at the market, feathers can be bought from fishing-tackle suppliers, while you may have plenty of flowers, leaves and twigs in your own back garden.

Once the materials are gathered, let them be your inspiration. The key to success is very often simplicity. If in doubt, use a generous amount of a single material for a homogenous look, rather than trying to create something complicated using too many different shapes, colours and textures.

All the projects in this book are very easy to do and do not require complicated skills or specialized tools. They're designed to inspire even more than to instruct, and to help you bring the joy of the countryside into your own home.

WORKING WITH NATURE

Much of the joy of working with nature comes from making something that celebrates her beauty, rather than obscures it. The aim of the projects in this book is to retain the look and character of the materials, rather than to fuss them with complicated techniques and methods. Having said that, there are some basic skills you need to know in order to prepare and preserve some of the materials. Eggs need to be blown if they are to last more than a week; shells need to be cleaned, and there are various ways to preserve flowers and leaves. Over the next few pages you will find all the basic skills that will enable you to make everything in this book. There is also a feather directory to help you plan what to ask for at the fishing-tackle shop!

LEFT: Glorious tangles of flower stems support the flat heads of yarrow that has been cut, bunched and hung to dry.

HARVESTING AND GLEANING

One of the most inspiring aspects of wildcrafts must be collecting the materials. A walk in the woods may produce some wonderful gnarled twigs or straight and slender new shoots. As well as shells, a beach walk will offer driftwood, honed into elegant smooth, weathered grey shapes by the ocean. There may be wonderfully rusted old nails, pebbles sandwashed into graceful shapes, or even, the prize of all prizes, a stone with a hole worn by the waves. Early spring is one of the best times to comb the beach for nature's treasures. The storms and violent seas of winter bring up the most bounty, and in spring there are fewer people on the beach to collect the best pieces. But as the spring turns into summer and temperatures begin to rise, you are likely to be spending more time by the sea. Even if there is more competition, there is still plenty of treasure to be found.

Search out pretty shells and pebbles, and let the children fill their buckets to bring home souvenirs of their holidays. However, do be aware that in some countries it is illegal to take any shell from the beach, even if its inhabitant has long since departed. Even shingle is seen as part of the heritage in its natural habitat. The odd pebble is unlikely to be missed, but bag-loads, taken for whatever reason, could be unlawful.

Handling wild birds' nests or eggs is also illegal in most countries. The mere touch of a human hand is enough reason for a parent to abandon the nest in some cases, endangering the survival of rare species. However, the broken shells of hatched wild birds' eggs make for fine pickings, and can be the raw material, for example, for a miniature mosaic. One of the easiest

LEFT: Pebbles that are displayed in jars of water will regain their sheen and depth of colour.

ABOVE: Always keep an eye out for pieces of driftwood on your visits to the beach.

and definitely ecologically friendly ways to create the look of wild birds' eggs is to use quails' eggs, which are stocked by some supermarkets or in specialist food shops.

Wild flowers, many of which are protected, can be another trap for the wildcrafter. You're usually safe cutting one or two stems of abundant flowers such as dandelions, buttercups or daisies, but if you want to pick a lot of wild flowers for use indoors, it is safer to buy a packet of wild flower seed and grow them yourself.

Some garden plants, such as varieties of herbs, have not altered much from their wild state. These are still grown for their flavour and perfume rather than for their appearance, and so still retain wild looks even if they are cultivated.

There are other wonderful materials that can be found in your own garden. If you soft-pruned in the autumn, early spring is the time to hard-prune some species. Buddleia is a prime example. Those long straight branches can be cut right down to within 15cm/6in of the ground in early spring, providing a harvest of twigs that can be transformed into useful containers or frames as well as delightful seasonal wreaths.

Twigs, as well as boughs and logs, can also be found in woods and forests, and woodland walks are ideal for gleaning all kinds of inspirational material. Never strip the trees of anything, though; only take what you find on the forest floor, even in summer rain and fresh winds will release leaves and twigs from the trees.

RIGHT: The long thin shoots of spring make a useful craft material. If you can't collect them in an environmentally friendly way, a good florist will be able to order them for you.

DECORATING EGGS

 Although eggs are traditionally seen as symbolic of Easter, their pleasing shape makes them a delightful decorative form all year round. Having said that, spring is the right time to buy the eggs of some of the more unusual domestic fowl, if they are available, such as duck and goose. See what you can find in specialist shops.

If you want to serve coloured eggs for breakfast on Easter morning, the best solution is to buy edible egg dye, which is usually available at this time of year. Alternatively, make up a strong solution of food colouring and colour the eggs that way. Although many colours can be obtained using traditional vegetable dyes, the pigments can be difficult to get hold of, and the results are variable. However, one of the easiest, effective and most reliable vegetable dyes is produced by onion skins.

ONION SKIN EGGS

Peel about four onions and reserve them for another use. Put the skins, with about six eggs, into a pan of boiling water. Add a handful of salt as a fixative. Boil the eggs for about ten

RIGHT: Onion skins lend glorious coppery tones to ordinary eggs. These have been dyed with both ordinary onions and those with red skins.

ABOVE: Use brown or red onions to dye eggs; both need plenty of salt to fix the colour.

minutes until they have taken on the colour from the onion skins, then lift them out of the water, rinse them in clear water, and place them on paper towels to drain. Finally, rub a little vegetable oil on to the shells to create a sheen.

DYEING EGGS FOR DECORATION

Dyeing eggs that are not going to be eaten allows you to choose from a wider colour range. One of the most effective ways is to use fabric dyes, which offer a glorious palette of colours. These eggs will not be suitable for eating, as the chemicals in the dye can work themselves through the porous shell into the eggs. However, they make wonderful decorative accessories for Easter, and

if they are blown to remove all their contents, they can be kept almost indefinitely. It is best to dye the eggs before blowing them as the weight of their contents keeps the egg in the dye. Hollow shells would float on the top of the solution and dye unevenly, and weighting the fragile eggs down would easily damage them.

Make up the fabric dye with boiling water according to the manufacturer's instructions. You will need to add salt – often a surprising amount, but don't scrimp, as the salt is a fixative. Pour the dye into a bowl, then lower in as many eggs as will fit into the bowl. Once the eggs have taken on the colour, lift them out with a metal spoon, rinse under clear water, then leave to drain on paper towels. Keep an eye on the

BELOW: For hygiene reasons, it is important to rinse the inside of the blown eggs thoroughly.

ABOVE: Domestic goose and duck eggs are larger alternatives to hen's eggs.

eggs while they are in the dye, lifting them out to check their progress regularly. The dye will take more quickly with the first batch of eggs than with subsequent batches.

TO BLOW EGGS

Use a large upholstery or darning needle to make a hole in each end of the egg. Carefully enlarge one hole, then, holding the egg over a bowl, blow through the small hole until all the contents of the egg have been forced out. Cover the small hole with your finger and hold the large hole under a running tap to part-fill the eggshell with water. Shake the egg to rinse it, then blow the water out. Repeat until the water is clean.

SHELLS

The unique combination of a tough resilience designed to withstand the stormiest of seas and a delicate appearance has given shells an enduring appeal for artists and craftspeople alike. Their forms can be as simple as the basic dish-shape of a mussel or clam, or as complex as the intricate spiky murex. Their colours span a wonderful palette of silvery greys and tans through to coral, pink and creamy shades.

You can use shells in many different decorative ways, by gluing them to hard surfaces with strong adhesive or sewing them on to soft furnishings in fringes.

BELOW: Clean shells thoroughly using a small kitchen knife, then soak them in a strong solution of washing-up liquid. The shells can then be left out in the garden to weather them further.

ABOVE: Drilling holes is a fiddly business, but can be done using a fine bit on an electric drill.

First, however, the shells need to be collected in an ecologically sensitive way. The best source of mussel and scallop shells is the fishmonger. After cooking and eating the shellfish, the shells will need to be thoroughly cleaned. Scrape off any debris with a sharp knife, then soak in a strong solution of washing-up liquid.

Shells can always be found on the beach, but remember that it is illegal even to remove them from the shore in some countries, and you could well find yourself facing a hefty fine if you tried to take one through customs. Craft and gift shops often sell bags of shells, many of which are labelled as ecologically collected. Another useful source of shells is to buy made-up items such as necklaces and tablemats, for cutting up

and recycling. These are often inexpensive, and the advantage is that the shells will already be drilled with tiny holes and ready to use. If you need to drill holes yourself, use an ordinary electric drill fitted with a very fine bit. To "sew" the shells, use strong and discreet nylon thread.

When securing shells with adhesive, choose one that is very strong, thick and fast-setting, such as hot glue applied with a glue gun. Most shells have very little flat surface and need to be "bedded in" to allow contact along at least some of their contours.

BELOW: It is not difficult to find shell necklaces and other inexpensive shell products in craft and gift shops specializing in items from the Far East. These are a good source for ready-drilled shells. Simply snip the thread and slip off the shells, sorting them into different kinds as you go.

PRESSING FLOWERS AND LEAVES

A wonderful way of capturing the beauty of the growing season is to press flowers and leaves. You could buy a special flower press, but it is easy to make your own press using an artist's watercolour book and blotting paper or tissue.

Leaves are particularly suitable for pressing, since they are already flat. The most suitable flowers for pressing are those that are also fairly flat, such as primroses, pansies, hydrangea florets and buttercups. Flowers with tightly-packed petals, such as roses, are not such good candidates. If you wish to capture the beauty of multi-petalled flowers, press individual petals. This works very well with larger petalled flowers, such as Iceland poppies.

BELOW: Flat leaves make ideal pressing material and are very easy to handle.

ABOVE: Two-dimensional flowers are perfect to press.

TO PRESS FLOWERS AND LEAVES

The best time to pick flowers and leaves to be pressed is around mid-morning while they are still fresh, before the sun has had time to scorch them and after the dew has evaporated. Pick plenty, looking for an assortment of sizes. Even a single plant can offer a variety of young and more mature leaves of different sizes, and you may sometimes want to choose groups of leaves, rather than individual ones. Carefully remove

any damaged parts so that you have only the perfect-looking specimens. Lay some of the plant material on the first layer of blotting paper or soft tissue, carefully flattening each piece. If stems holding groups of leaves can be encouraged to take on a graceful curve, this will be useful. Lay another sheet of blotting paper on top of the flowers and leaves, turn over the page and repeat with the next layer.

The flowers and leaves need to be left in the press until every droplet of moisture has been absorbed. When you can lift them up and they retain the same shape without flopping at all, they are ready. Some pieces will be ready before others, but even when they are dry, it is best to leave them in the book until you use them.

BELOW: Press more material than you need so you have a choice when making up your designs.

DRYING FLOWERS

The three-dimensional shape and, to a certain extent, the colour of some flowers can be preserved by drying. This way, a glut of summer flowers need not go to waste: use dried flowers immediately for everlasting displays or store them to use in the autumn when the nights draw in and there's more time for indoor pursuits.

Some flowers are better suited to drying than others, and one of the best ways of discovering which ones these are is to touch them while they are still growing. Those with a natural dryness will preserve well. If you become a dried flower enthusiast, it may be worth considering growing your own crop. The seeds of many varieties

BELOW: Strip off the leaves before bunching up the flowers to dry.

ABOVE: Bind flowers to be dried in elastic bands that will continue to grip the stems as they dry and shrink.

are inexpensive, and may even be sold as "Everlasting Varieties", or "Flowers for Drying". Easy to grow, the challenge is to keep up with the demands of harvesting even a small patch, as they must be picked as soon as they are ready.

TO DRY FLOWERS

The flowers should be picked around the middle of the morning on the first day they are fully open. This is important because, as they

mature, the colour dissipates and, in the case of perfumed plants, so does the aroma.

As soon as you have picked the flowers, remove all the leaves, as these don't dry well and they retain moisture, slowing the drying process. Next, gather the flowers into small bunches and secure with an elastic band, which – unlike string

FLOWERS THAT DRY EASILY

flowers from the onion family (*allium*)

artichoke and cardoon (*cynara*)

Chinese lanterns (*physalis*)

cornflower (*centaurea cyanus*)

eucalyptus

globe thistle (*echinops*)

helichrysum

hydrangea

kangaroo paw (*anigozanthos*)

love-in-a-mist (*nigella*)

bells of Ireland (*mollucella*)

cape honey flower (*protea*)

statice (*phsylliostachys*)

yarrow (*achillea*)

or twine – will tighten as the stems dry out and shrink, continuing to hold them safely. Hang up the bunches of flowers on hooks in the ceiling or high on walls, with plenty of space between each one, in a dry area where there is plenty of circulating air. The outside of the staircase is fine if you have nowhere more suitable.

RIGHT: Hang up bunches of yarrow in midsummer, before their wonderful golden plate-like blooms begin to turn brown, and their colour will be retained all through the coming winter.

A FEATHER DIRECTORY

Feathers are a delightful material for creating all manner of trimmings and decorations. Soft and light, they range in size from those that are delicate and downy to the long, graceful quills that adorn the tails of some of the more showy birds. The male plumage offers the most dazzling array of colours, though the less flamboyant shades of mocha, beige, tan and whisper grey, found on many wild and domestic fowl, can often be used to create the most winsome of wild effects.

It is always easy to pick up the odd feather in the countryside, especially in areas where there are plenty of pheasant, grouse and wild duck.

BELOW: Mallard duck wing feathers show a handsome flash of iridescent blue.

Alternatively you could try breeders of fancy poultry, or local farms that rear chickens, geese and ducks on a free range basis, but by far the best are fishing-tackle suppliers, who sell a variety of feathers for fly-tying.

RIGHT: Even the downiest peacock feathers gleam with remarkable colours at their tips.

BELOW: Male pheasants' feathers offer plenty of contrast between their soft grey down and fiery orange tips, and are more versatile than larger showy quills.

ABOVE: Golden sebright bantam feathers come in a glorious tan, outlined smartly in black. The quills are a particularly useful size.

ABOVE: Teal ducks wear smart grey stripes. Their feathers have an elegant pointed tip that lends a chic finished look.

ABOVE: Guinea fowl feathers come in almost unbelievable spots, making them one of the most delightful to work with.

BELOW: The pretty shape and coffee-and-cream colouring of female mallard feathers make an attractive combination.

BELOW: The palest grey and cream topped by a strip of black and tan makes the French partridge feather one of the smartest available.

BELOW: The tiny feathers of the wild partridge come in subtle stripes of greys and tans and, although fiddly to work with, make beautiful finished pieces.

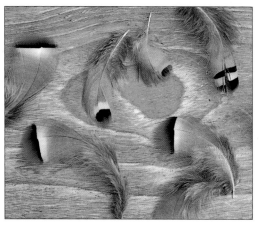

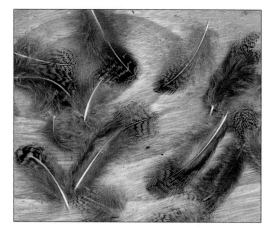

SWEET EARLY SPRING

ABOVE: Fruit trees are generous with their blossom, producing enough for us to share without spoiling the show left on the tree.

LEFT: Nest-building is symbolic both of spring and of new life. Create a seasonal decoration using domestic quail's eggs for a wild look.

Spring blooms and blossoms must be the most welcome of the year as they seem to burst from bare earth and burgeon from naked twigs. Every year they appear, full of enthusiasm and optimism, just as we know they will. Yet every year they surprise and thrill us with their arrival. In Germany it is traditional to cut branches of

BELOW: Diminutive speckled quail's eggs and soft pussy willow are both symbolic of early spring.

ABOVE: Pure white eggs and pear blossom make a simple seasonal display.

larch, pussy willow and catkins to decorate with wooden eggs for Easter. When they are first brought indoors, many of the branches look unpromisingly bare, but in the unfamiliar warmth they burst into life, symbolizing the annual rite of new birth.

In early spring there is an air of expectancy, even in the bare trees. There is a feeling of anticipation as the air softens and birds collect twigs for nest-building. Fruit-tree boughs brought inside not only echo this, but have a ruggedly wild look. Don't try too hard to tame

them; just settle them into large metal or stoneware containers of water to enjoy their wildness. At this time of year twigs and branches of other trees make ideal material for making more permanent items than floral displays. Some species, such as willow and dogwood, send out long, straight, pliable shoots in spring that are highly versatile for all kinds of crafts.

BELOW: Crisp greens and clear whites offer a refreshing colour scheme for the new season.

In the early months of the year, before the herbaceous perennials and annuals appear, most of the flowers have a charming simplicity. Abundant white and pink fruit blossoms dance like ballerinas in the trees, and swathes of primary-coloured early bulbs seem to be putting on an extra effort to make up for the earlier barren months of winter.

Leaves make an extra effort, too. Even evergreens, that have kept their dark green mantle throughout the winter, push out new emerald shoots, which appear like dappled light on the plants. If you cut the leaves very carefully, gleaning such treasures at this time of the year does little damage to the plant as there's a long growing season ahead: indeed, a judicious amount of trimming will simply encourage them into a bushier habit.

The succulence of the new growth allows no opportunities for pressing or drying, almost as a protest against anyone trying to harness its vigour. So gather the boughs and the flowers and simply stand them in containers, or work them into garlands and wreaths for times of celebration. Enjoy them now, while they have the freshness of new life in spring.

RIGHT: Branches of apple and pear blossom look glorious in huge stoneware and metal containers.

NEST TABLE DECORATION

In early spring, when there are still few flowers available for cutting, a nest makes a most delightful seasonal display. Tiny speckled quail's eggs, which can be bought at delicatessens or some supermarkets, lend a genuinely wild look.

MATERIALS

8 willow sticks 15cm/6in long
secateurs (pruners)
willow wreath, 15cm/6in in diameter
raffia
scissors
large plastic bag
sphagnum moss
small feathers
5 quail's eggs

1 The willow sticks make up the base of the nest, so trim them to fit across the wreath.

2 Use short lengths of raffia to tie the willow sticks to the base of the wreath.

3 Turn the "nest" right side up. Cut a circle of sheet from the plastic bag to line the nest, making it large enough to cover the bottom and go a little way up the sides too.

4 Tease out enough moss to line the nest. Looser moss has a more natural look.

5 Add a few feathers, carefully lay the quail's eggs in the nest, and finish with a few more feathers.

NOTE
It is illegal to take eggs from the wild.
Only use the eggs of domesticated fowl.

DAFFODIL AND BOX DISPLAY

 Using plants, rather than cut flowers, makes for wonderfully organic displays that can be used inside or out. They look just as lovely in a living or dining room as outside on a windowsill, doorstep or garden table. Here, cheerful nodding narcissi are set off by young emerald green box plants. The narcissi can be planted in the autumn and kept in a cool dark place until the shoots appear in the spring, or you can buy them in pots at a florist or market when they are in bud and ready to bloom. The display will far outlast any cut flowers. As the flowers fade, they can be replaced by later varieties of narcissi, grape hyacinths (*muscari*) or tulips. In early summer, plant the box outside in the garden.

MATERIALS
watering can
8 young box plants (*Buxus sempervirens*)
5 narcissi bulbs (*Narcissus* 'Tête-à-Tête') in bud
8 small terracotta pots
compost (soil mix)
large terracotta pot
sphagnum moss

LEFT: The lime-green of the newest box leaves contrasts strikingly with the older, darker leaves, giving the impression of sun and shade.

NOTE
Potted plants need plenty of water. The compost soon dries out, especially on a dry, windy day. When the top of the compost (soil mix) feels dry to the touch, water well until the water comes out of the bottom of the pot to ensure it is wet through.

1 Water the plants well and allow them to drain for at least an hour.

2 Re-pot the young box plants in the small terracotta pots, taking care not to damage the roots. Firm in extra compost (soil mix) if needed.

3 Re-pot the bulbs all together in the large terracotta pot, firming in extra compost if needed.

4 Dress the tops of the pots with moss, then arrange the small pots around the large one. Water well, and water again whenever the surface feels dry to the touch.

DOGWOOD HEART

In early spring, the young burgundy shoots of dogwood are particularly prominent before the shrub produces its foliage. Mature shrubs produce a mass of branches, a few of which can easily be pruned without affecting the overall shape. Use the branches as soon as you can after cutting, while they are still full of sap and pliable, to make this charming wall decoration.

MATERIALS

generous bundle of dogwood shoots (*Cornus alba*)

florist's wire

secateurs (pruners)

raffia

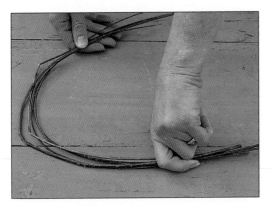

1 Select two bundles of five long shoots. Very carefully, bend each bundle into a large U-shape, easing the shoots as you go to avoid snapping them.

2 Hold the two U-shapes at right angles to each other to create a heart shape. Using the florist's wire, join the shapes together where they cross. You will need to keep easing the dogwood into position.

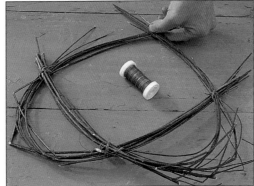

3 Wire the bottom point of the heart. Once you have established the shape of the heart, you may want to re-wire all the joints to hold them firmly in place. Trim any very long ends. You have now created the basic heart shape of the wreath.

4 Build on the basic shape, thickening it up by adding some finer and shorter shoots to the top and fixing them in place with wire. These will be more pliable than the original, larger ones.

5 Finish by binding all the joints with raffia. Make sure you cover all the wire. Finally, trim all the ends to neaten and to ensure a pretty finished shape.

FEATHER PICTURES

Feathers, simply mounted in picture frames, make original and effective decorations. The most successful compositions show a sympathy between frame and feathers, echoing their tones and keeping the proportions balanced. Most feathers look their best mounted on creamy or neutral paper – particularly handmade paper. Stick the feathers in place using the smallest dab of PVA (white) glue or high-tack craft adhesive.

BELOW: Gloriously fluffy and softly toned, a female mallard's feather looks delightful filling a simple beechwood frame.

ABOVE: Quills look wonderful when not trapped behind glass, as their aerodynamic quality lends an extra dimension, with the feather tip lifting clear of the mount. The simple piece of cotton string appears to tie the feather down, while the colour of the golden sebright bantam quill is echoed on the inner edge of the frame.

RIGHT: Neatly tailored male pheasant feathers look wonderful in ordered lines. Two large feathers with a matching pair of small ones on either side make a more interesting composition. The soft grey tones of the frame, recycled from an old barn door, are echoed in the downy part of the feathers.

SPRINGTIME WREATH

 Even a few sprigs of fruit blossom and pussy willow can be transformed into a lush seasonal wreath when teamed with the fresh new growth that brings added vigour to evergreens. The foliage here is rosemary, a profuse shrub that benefits from being cut back. Its fragrance awakens the senses, adding charm to the wreath.

MATERIALS
florist's foam ring, 20cm/8in in diameter
large bunch of young rosemary shoots
secateurs (pruners)
pussy willow *(Salix caprea)*
pear blossom

2 Push the rosemary into the foam ring, arranging it at an angle so it flows around the circle in one direction. Add the pussy willow, placing most of it at the top of the inside edge for impact.

1 Soak the florist's foam ring in water until it is completely soaked through. Cut the stems of rosemary into 15cm/6in pieces.

3 Place most of the pear blossom so that it covers the inside edge of the ring. Add a few blossoms to the outside. Fill any gaps with spare rosemary.

RIVETED LEAF NAPKIN RINGS

 Any large, leathery leaves can be quickly transformed into napkin rings. These are made from Fatsia japonica, an evergreen that puts on astounding growth in the spring, daily producing new five-fingered leaves. Riveting them together is both quick and easy, using a small riveting kit available at haberdashers.

MATERIALS
FOR EACH NAPKIN:
Fatsia japonica leaf, or similar
secateurs (pruners)
2 rivets
riveting pliers

2 Choose half grown leaves, as they still retain their sharp green shades and are at their most pliable. Cut off the stalks of the leaves you have selected.

1 Fold each napkin into a triangle and roll the ends into the middle.

3 Wrap the leaf around the napkin. Secure in position by riveting the sides together using riveting pliers.

TWIGGY TRAY

A tray of twigs is easy to make and surprisingly robust – all for the cost of a few strands of raffia. This tray is made from young willow shoots, but any twigs will do as long as they're fairly straight and of a similar thickness. The end result is wonderfully organic – perfect for outdoor drinks or snacks.

MATERIALS

raffia

about 60 young willow (or similar) shoots, 45cm/18in long

secateurs (pruners)

1 Fold a strand of raffia in half and place the end of one willow stick in the loop. Now bring the lower piece of raffia up and the upper piece down, enclosing the stick, and place the next stick in between the two lengths of raffia.

2 Bring the lower piece up and the upper piece down again to enclose the next stick, and position the third stick. You will find that you soon develop a twisting rhythm. Continue until you have woven in 44 sticks. Weave in three more lines of raffia about 9cm/3½ in apart down the length of the sticks and one near the other end, to create a firm mat for the base.

3 Cut eight sticks to fit the short sides of the tray base. Make the first side of the tray by laying down four full-length sticks at right angles to four of the shorter sticks. Tie the middle of a strand of raffia around one of the long sticks. Place one of the short sticks at right angles on top of this and tie that in. Continue until all eight sticks are used up and tie firmly.

4 Create the other three corners in the same way until you have made up a rectangular frame that will become the sides of the tray.

5 Place the frame over the base. Feed the raffia into the side of the base at the end of one of the lines. As before, work the two ends of raffia up the side and down again, tying them together at the bottom. Repeat wherever the frame meets the ends of the woven raffia on the base, and at two intervals along the short sides.

6 *To attach the short sides, fold a piece of raffia in half and feed one end from underneath the base between two sticks, over the lowest frame stick and back down between the sticks to meet the other end of the raffia. Tie underneath. Repeat between the next two sticks, over the lower frame stick, and down again.*

7 *Tie the two ends together again tightly. Continue in this way until the full width of the frame is tied to the base at one end. Repeat at the other end to complete.*

WILLOW AND FEATHER STAR

The natural tones of willow sticks and wild bird feathers harmonize beautifully and can very easily be transformed into endless wreaths and hangings. Light and airy in appearance, this delicate-looking star is much more robust than it first appears.

MATERIALS

secateurs (pruners)

18 willow sticks, about 40cm/16in long

raffia

scissors

high-tack craft glue

about 40 female pheasant feathers

BELOW: Two raffia-tied feathers add the finishing touch to each point of the star.

1 Using secateurs (pruners), trim the sticks roughly to length. Lay three bundles of three sticks on a surface to form a triangle. Use raffia to bind the corners.

2 Repeat to make a second triangle, using the rest of the sticks. Lay one triangle on top of the other to form a star and, using the raffia, bind the star together at all the points where the triangles cross.

3 Trim the ends of the sticks close to the raffia to neaten the shape.

4 Using the high-tack glue, stick the feathers to the inner hexagon of the star, wedging them between the sticks. To finish the points of the stars, tie pairs of feathers into V-shapes using raffia, then glue them into position.

MINI ALPINE SHELL GARDEN

Create an alpine shell garden in a shell-decorated container for an unusual window box or garden decoration. The garden needs to be planted in spring after the frosts and once planted, it will grow with very little attention, producing little flowers in the summer in return for the occasional watering. It will rest in the winter, ready to grow with renewed vigour in the following spring.

MATERIALS

wooden vegetable box
lime-green emulsion (latex) paint
paintbrush
glue gun and glue sticks
12 scallop shells
large plastic bag
scissors
compost (soil mix)
selection of larger shells
selection of about 8 alpine plants such as
houseleeks (*sempervivum*), sedum and saxifrage

2 Using the glue gun, attach scallop shells all around the sides of the box. Line the box with plastic cut from the bag, and make holes in it with scissors for drainage.

4 Remove one of the alpines from its pot and position it in the box. The roots can be wedged under a shell and bedded well into the compost.

1 Paint the box with lime-green emulsion (latex) paint and allow to dry. As this is really an indoor paint, it will weather down over the year to softer tones. Water the plants well and allow to drain.

3 Add a generous layer of compost (soil mix) to the box, then arrange the larger shells on top.

5 Repeat with the rest of the plants, arranging them so the different greens set each other off. Until the plants grow to fill the box, you can add a few more small shells to cover the bare earth.

DECORATIVE BLOSSOM

 The joyous sight of dainty blossom and delicate leaves bursting from twigs is hard to resist as we bring home spring's first blooms. But sometimes the twigs are slightly bare and could do with a little decorative help. Use the blossoms themselves to create an eyecatching show.

ABOVE: Soak a small square of florist's foam and place in the nest, or make a little nest from tangled moss. Push sprigs of the blossom and other material into the foam or moss nest and decorate with pussy willow.

LEFT: Use the florist's wire to fix the nest to the branches of an arrangement of twigs.

RIGHT: Where the twigs of blossom have a bare patch, fill the space by attaching small glass jars suspended from strings and filled to the brim with spare blossoms.

BELOW: Blossom can look wonderful cut short and arranged in shallow bowls. Any left-over sprigs can float gently on the top of the water.

43

HEARTS AND FLOWERS

The lush abundance of ornamental cherry blossom needs no decoration or embellishment, but in a simple glass container its woody stems look charming tied and decorated with a raffia heart. This can then be complemented by more hearts, hung in the branches.

MATERIALS

garden wire

wire cutters

raffia

ornamental cherry blossom

glass vase

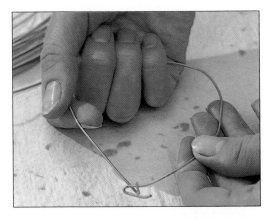

1 Cut a length of wire about 30cm/12in long, make a hook in each end and link the hooks together. Make a dip in the middle of the wire for the top of the little heart shape.

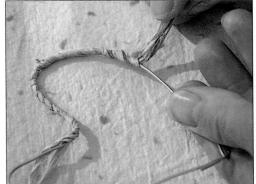

2 Starting at the dip and leaving a tail free for tying up at the end, begin to bind the wire with the raffia.

LEFT: Raffia is a natural material that is quite happy under water, and this also magnifies the heart.

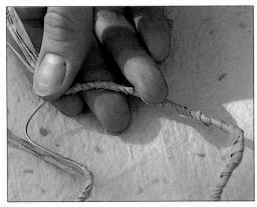

3 Take your time to bind the raffia, carefully winding it densely all around the heart, and pulling it taut as you go. Ensure that the wire is completely covered with the raffia.

4 When you get back to the top, tie the ends together firmly, then make a bow. Cut the cherry blossom branches to a length suitable for the container. Tie the branches into a bunch using raffia, then tie on the heart. Place the whole arrangment into a large vase.

QUICK SPRING DISPLAYS

The charm of spring flowers is their simplicity. Their shapes are generally uncomplicated, with straight stems and grass-like or succulent emerald-green leaves. The most pleasing way to display them is to fuss the flowers as little as possible – simply aim to find a complementary container, cut the stems to a length that flatters both flowers and container, then enjoy their natural charm. If in doubt about how long to cut the stems, a useful guide is to display them in a way that mimics the way they grow. Keep stems long and if they are branched, keep them that way. However you display them, remember to cut about 2.5cm/1in off the end of each stem just before putting them into the container to help the flowers take up the water.

LEFT: Pure white perfumed lilac teamed with fuller white pear blossom makes a lovely bouquet for a guest's bedroom. Tied with an old gold ribbon and set in a golden glass, it decorates a dressing table or bedside table delightfully, while exuding its glorious scent.

RIGHT: An old stoneware pitcher is the perfect receptacle for pussy willow, its soft tones complementing the muted grey tones of the branches. To retain the wild beauty of the willow, just cut a few branches and put them loosely in a container.

RIGHT: Snake's-head fritillary (Fritillaria meleagris) must be one of the most pleasing yet unfamiliar spring flowers. Their charming nodding heads, distinctively patterned with checks, and deep green grass-like leaves are a joy to behold both outside and in. Inside they look wonderful in verdigris containers. Leave their stems long, so the flower heads can dance in a crowd, much as they would in the wild. Add a bowlful of eggs to the display for a really seasonal look.

47

LATE SPRING EXUBERANCE

Here tulips bloom as they are told;
Unkempt about those hedges blows
An English unofficial rose.
RUPERT BROOKE (1887–1915)

ABOVE: *Chic checked eggs are fun and easy to do, making a smart spring decoration*
that will look good for the rest of the year too.

LEFT: *By late spring, the garden and countryside are full of the wild exuberance*
and colour of blooms and blossoms.

49

 The rich abundance of late spring fulfils the promise of the early months. Flowers with waxy petals, vibrant colours and rich perfumes lend nature a youthful exuberance that is the prelude to the full maturity of summer. Now is the time for celebration. Spring festivals are a hallmark of folk cultures in every part of the world where winter bites, and to mark them, symbols of new life are traditionally incorporated into arts and crafts. Eggs have been decorated and exchanged during spring since pagan times. Abundant flowers have always been cut and brought in from the fields.

In late spring, making up a posy of bright flowers enables you to appreciate them from a different perspective. One of the most successful and effective ways of treating cut spring flowers is to use a large bunch of just one kind in a suitable container. At this time of the year, the varieties come into season in rapid succession, so use those that are most plentiful each

LEFT: Auriculas are one of the most charming late spring flowers: the Victorians celebrated them in paintings, and even displayed them in their own velvet-lined theatres. It is just as rewarding today to display them prominently in pots so you can really enjoy their exquisite colouring.

week, and you'll have a changing display with impact. By choosing flowers at the peak of their season you'll not only have plenty of material, you'll also have a less expensive bill at the florist.

Don't be too hasty to discard flowers that are going past their best. Many look beautiful in their last days, and that is part of the joy of working with natural materials. Tulips, for

BELOW: Late spring is traditionally the time to decorate eggs, the symbol of new life.

ABOVE: In folklore, lily-of-the-valley, with its delicious scent and delicate flowers, symbolizes the return of hope.

example, start off with sharp obelisk-like buds in strong colours. As they open, the shape loosens into a much more casual look, and the colours begin to soften. Towards the end of their life, they flamboyantly show their centres, and eventually the colours take on glorious muted tones. Theirs is a wonderful moving show, as they continue to grow even after they are cut. Alternatively, the sculptural quality of many spring flowers can be used to create dazzling architectural floral displays for special celebrations. With stalks cut short and blooms densely packed, flowers take on different personalities. Displays retain their original form throughout their life, but appear to become denser as the petals open and grow.

Feathers are another delightful springtime material to work with, reminiscent of downy nest linings. They come in a glorious range of natural colours from whites and greys to beiges, browns and black, and can be used as trimmings for home decorations and to make accessories.

51

LEAF-STENCILLED EGGS

Eggs and new leaves are two powerful symbols of spring. Here, they have been combined in an exquisite yet easy-to-do decoration. Do not attempt to eat the eggs once decorated.

MATERIALS

cold-water fabric dye

salt

large white eggs

metal spoon

kitchen paper

all-purpose glue

leaves

stencil brush

stencil paint

newspaper

BELOW: The top coat gives a stippled finished effect.

1 Make up the dye according to the manufacturer's instructions, and add the specified amount of salt. Lower an egg into the dye. Check the egg after a few minutes, and if it has reached the colour you want, take it out with a metal spoon, rinse in cold water and allow it to drain on kitchen paper.

2 When the egg is dry, wipe it over with kitchen paper. Place a thin film of glue on the back of a leaf and smooth the leaf on to the shell.

3 Dip the tip of the stencil brush into the stencil paint and dab off the excess on newspaper or kitchen paper. The brush should be almost dry. Gently apply a thin film of paint to the egg, using a stabbing motion to give a speckled effect that allows the colour of the undercoat to show through.

4 When the paint is dry to the touch (it will dry quickly), carefully peel off the leaf. Allow the paint to dry fully before arranging the eggs in a bowl.

SPRING POSIES

 It is always lovely to give and to receive flowers, and all the more so if they're arranged in a posy tied with a pretty ribbon. The word posy originates from the sixteenth-century "poesy", another word for the poem or motto that was written on the paper wrapped around the flowers. Soon, for the very well-chaperoned

LEFT: *Blue hyacinths (constancy) and gentler-toned grape hyacinths always look wonderful against the vibrant emerald leaves of the latter.*

BELOW: *The appearance of fragrant pure white blooms of lily-of-the-valley, set against broad lime-green leaves, indicates the long-awaited warmer weather, and in the language of flowers, the return of happiness. Tied with the palest yellow ribbon striped with lime, they make a charming gift.*

54

ABOVE: The sharp green alchemilla leaves setting off this posy hold no particular meaning in the language of flowers, though the auriculas indicate beauty.

RIGHT: In Victorian times this delightful posy of forget-me-nots and anemones would have conveyed the sad message that a true love had been forsaken.

Victorians, the flowers themselves came to symbolize emotions and took the place of the poems, so the language of flowers developed.

With both sad and joyous emotions so easily conveyed, it is unfortunate that this fascinating language is no longer part of our culture. These pretty posies are some examples of spring messages that might have been sent and received in Victorian times.

BLUE AND WHITE EGGS

 Blue and white patterns always look fresh, and this is a chic and easy decoration for eggs. The design is created by sticking on small squares of masking tape, then stippling on the colour using a stencil brush. This group of different sized eggs has been decorated with different-sized checks for variety. The width of the paper strips determines the size of the checks. Do not attempt to eat the eggs once decorated.

MATERIALS
scissors

masking tape

selection of blown white eggs

stencil brush

stencil paint

newspaper or kitchen paper

1 Cut several strips of masking tape.

2 Cut squares of masking tape from the strips and stick them to each egg in chequerboard fashion.

3 It is best to start by making a band three squares wide all around the length of the egg, leaving the narrow end free so that it will be a solid colour. Next, fill in as much of the rest of the shell around this band as possible. At the wide end you will need to adjust the size and positioning of the squares to fit, even cutting triangles if appropriate.

4 Dip the tip of the stencil brush into the paint, dab off the excess on newspaper or kitchen paper, then apply the paint to the egg using a gentle dabbing motion for a subtle stippled effect.

5 Allow the paint to dry completely, then carefully peel off the masking tape squares. Don't be rough when removing the tape as the eggs are very fragile; it would be very unfortunate if you broke one at this last stage of the project.

FEATHER CURTAIN FRINGE

 Elegant translucent sheer curtains can be given a delightful trim of feathers, sewn in place with glass beads. Choose the downiest feathers you can find, teaming their tones with those of the curtains. These have been fixed to crisp, pure cotton organdie curtains. The fabric has plenty of body and hangs well at the window, providing a great base for the feathers. The feathers are sewn on behind the curtain, with a tiny glass button on top that makes both for a neat finish and adds a charming decorative touch.

MATERIALS
teal duck feathers

small glass beads

sheer curtain

needle

matching sewing thread

scissors

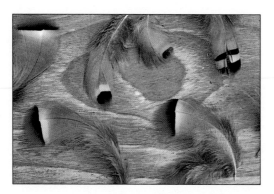

ABOVE: The light and airy teal duck feathers have a smart striped pattern that echoes the elegance of the organdie curtain.

LEFT: Teal duck feathers do give a distinctive finish to the curtain, but if you find it difficult to find them, adapt whatever is available. For example, you could use French partridge feathers such as these, or male pheasant feathers instead.

1 *Allow one feather and one bead for every 5cm/2in of curtain edging. Make a knot in the thread and take a neat stitch at the back of the curtain at the bottom outside edge of the curtain.*

2 *Pierce the feather quill with the needle and bring the quill down the thread. Hold in position against the back of the curtain edge.*

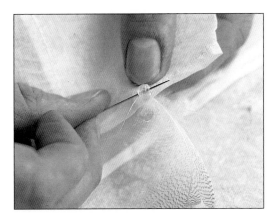

3 Bring the needle to the front of the curtain and thread on a bead. Pass the needle through to the back again, over the feather and back up to the front, through the bead and down again.

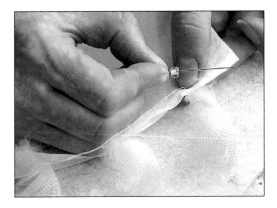

4 Continue in this way until both bead and feather are firmly stitched to the curtain. Secure the end of the thread at the back before attaching the next feather, 5cm/2in away along the curtain edge. Repeat until the fringe is complete.

DECOUPAGE EGGS

 The art of paper-cutting has a long tradition in Switzerland, where they use it to make greetings cards and pictures. This technique can be combined with the Victorian art of decoupage – decorating surfaces using cut-out motifs – to create enchanting decorated eggs that don't demand intricate paintbrush skills. This technique really isn't difficult, though it can be fiddly. Make sure you have some really sharp embroidery scissors. Also, use wallpaper paste as it is slow-drying and allows you to move the motifs around until you are happy with the position. Do not attempt to eat the eggs once decorated.

MATERIALS
sharp-pointed scissors
recycled paper in a selection of colours
paperclips
craft knife
cutting mat
pinking shears
blown white eggs
wallpaper paste
acrylic matt varnish
small varnish brush

RIGHT: Display the eggs in a glass jar for an orginal springtime gift.

1 Cut a piece of coloured paper to about 20 x 15cm/8 x 6in and fold it in half. Trace or photocopy the template from the back of the book, secure it to the paper with paperclips and cut round it. Cut out the wings, the eyes and between the legs. With pinking shears, cut two strips of different-coloured paper, 3mm/⅛ in wide and long enough to fit around the egg. With scissors, cut a similar strip in the first colour.

2 Make up the wallpaper paste according to the manufacturer's instructions. Using a finger, smear the surface of the egg and the back of the motifs with wallpaper paste, taking care not to let any of the paste get on to the front of the paper. Position one bird motif on each side of the egg.

3 Smear a little wallpaper paste on the edging strips and position these lengthways around the egg between the motifs. Trim the strips to length if necessary.

4 *Allow the egg to dry completely — preferably overnight — then brush on a thin coat of acrylic matt varnish. Allow to dry completely.*

BELOW: *These eggs also look very attractive displayed in a shallow dish.*

AURICULA DISPLAY

 Plant up a miniature garden in a bowl to make a delightful spring display, adding some tiny quail's eggs as a symbol of new birth. Auriculas have been used as the centrepiece of this arrangement. Their wonderful velvety flowers look as if they have been hand-painted, and deserve to be brought indoors for a while so that they can be appreciated at close quarters. Here, they are set off by cheerful, royal blue forget-me-nots. Choose vibrant colours and tiny flowers to provide a delightful contrast.

MATERIALS

watering can

6 auricula plants *(Primula auricula)*

10 forget-me-not plants

compost (soil mix)

large enamel bowl

sphagnum moss

6 quail's eggs

RIGHT: Nineteenth-century enthusiasts bred auriculas in quite astounding colours, from the soft watercolour shades used in the display or burgundies like this one to unusual varieties with green and even black petals.

1 Water the plants well and let them drain for an hour. Spread a layer of compost (soil mix) in the bottom of the bowl, then remove the auriculas from their pots and place them in the middle of the bowl. The tops of the rootballs should be about 4cm/1½ in below the rim of the bowl.

2 Next, empty out a forget-me-not plant and position it near to the edge of the bowl. Repeat with the rest of the forget-me-not plants. Carefully fill between all the plants with handfuls of compost, pressing it down well. Spread a thin layer of compost on top of the surface to make it level.

3 Dress the top of the pot with moss. Water well. Add the eggs. Water again when the surface feels dry to the touch, but do not overwater.

ABOVE: Tiny buttery-coloured violas would make a charming alternative to the auriculas.

TIP
This is a temporary display. Once the plants have finished blooming, the forget-me-nots, which are annuals, can be discarded, but if you would like forget-me-nots in the garden next year, put the container outside to allow them to self-seed. The auriculas can be planted out in the garden in moist but well-drained soil. Spread grit around the base of the plants to discourage slugs.

TULIP URN

 Tulips are fantastic flowers to work with. They have a wonderful sculptural quality and offer an endless choice of colour. These flaming red and yellow parrot tulips take on an almost architectural quality when teamed with a rusted urn. Wonderful whether it is kept inside or out, this display is easy to make, yet sufficiently striking for even the grandest occasion.

MATERIALS
florist's foam ball to fit urn
urn, about 18cm/7in diameter
large plastic bag
scissors
about 40 parrot tulips

BELOW: Parrot tulips come in wonderful rich tones, reminiscent of old Dutch paintings.

1 Thoroughly soak the florist's foam ball in water and allow to drain. Line the urn with a sheet of plastic cut from a large bag.

2 Cut the tulip stems to within about 2.5cm/1in of the flower head and arrange a line of tulips over the top of the ball. Space them so there is room for the flowers to open.

3 Fill in one side of the ball with tulips before beginning on the other. As you make successive rows, make sure that although there is room for the tulips to open, there is no florist's foam showing. The foam should hold enough water to keep the flowers fresh for several days, or even up to a week.

TIP

Making up fresh-flower topiaries uses a lot of material. Keep the costs down by using flowers that are at the peak of their season so you can avoid scrimping on the quantity. If you can't get enough blooms, aim to make a smaller topiary.

WILD BARLEY RING

Search any patch of long grass in late spring and you'll find wild barley growing in abundance. You don't even need to be in the country – the barley used for this wreath was found on open ground in a city, growing around trees where the grass had been left unmown.

MATERIALS
about 2.4m/8ft garden wire
florist's tape
wild barley

2 Make bundles of six ears of barley, cutting the stems to about 5cm/2in, and bind with florist's tape.

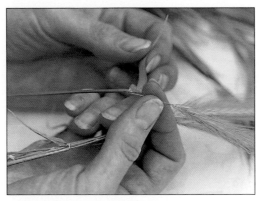

3 Bind the first bundle to the outside of the wire ring using the florist's tape. Place the next bundle on the inside of the ring, overlapping the stems of the first bundle, and bind. Place the third bundle on the outside of the wire, overlapping the second, and bind. Continue to bind the wire in this way until the ring is covered completely.

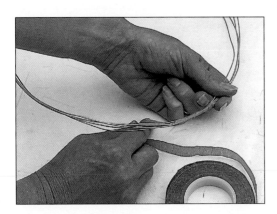

1 Make a circle about 18cm/7in in diameter, using several thicknesses of wire, and bind it all the way round with florist's tape.

FEATHER LAMPSHADES

 The natural colours of wild fowl feathers beautifully complement the smartest of cream-coloured interiors. Use them to trim simple cream coolie lampshades, choosing feathers with pretty shapes and markings to complement your design. Here, feathers of similar colours are used in different ways to create very different looks.

MATERIALS

scissors

ribbon or braid

small coolie lampshade

high-tack craft glue

small male pheasant feathers

1 Cut the ribbon or braid to fit the lower circumference of the lampshade, allowing a little extra for ease, and lay it on a flat surface. Place a spot of glue on the end of a feather and position it so that the end lies in the middle of the width of the ribbon. Place the next feather about 2.5cm/1in away from the first, and repeat to the end of the ribbon.

LEFT AND OPPOSITE: The simplest solutions can often be the most beautiful. Here, female mallard feathers seemingly "float" around the top and bottom of the lampshade. They have been glued securely just along their spines, so that the delicate down is free to move in the slightest breeze.

2 Run a line of glue along the length of the ribbon.

3 Fix the feathered edge of the ribbon to the bottom of the lampshade and turn the free edge to the inside of the shade. Repeat at the top of the lampshade, taking in tucks in the ribbon where necessary.

4 *Finish by carefully sticking another length of ribbon to the inside of the top to neaten.*

LOVE-IN-A-MIST OBELISK

This perky arrangement of love-in-a-mist would make a delightful table decoration for a wedding or engagement party. Make a huge one for the centrepiece, or several individual ones like this, setting one at each table, or if there aren't too many people, a tiny one for each guest. The lime-green of this tall, elegant painted terracotta pot perfectly complements the foliage, though blue or lilac would make good alternatives.

MATERIALS

florist's foam block
painted terracotta long Tom pot
kitchen knife
9 scabious
scissors
3 stems bupleurum
12 love-in-a-mist (*nigella*)
florist's reel wire

1 *Thoroughly soak the florist's foam block and drain. Press the rim of the container down on to the foam, then cut around the indented circle with a kitchen knife. Shape the top of the foam into an obelisk.*

LEFT: *Love-in-a-mist is one of the most satisfying summer annuals, with its pretty feathery leaves and simple blue flowers. Best of all, the more you pick them the more they bloom.*

2 *Place the foam in the container. Arrange two lines of scabious over the top of the obelisk to quarter it. Cut off the larger flower heads of the bupleurum to make a line around the rim of the pot.*

3 *Cut the love-in-a-mist stems close to the flower heads. Pass a short length of florist's reel wire through each stem and twist.*

4 *Fill the quarters between the scabious with the wired love-in-a-mist flower heads. Make sure the stem ends pierce the florist's foam, so they can take in the water and will last much longer.*

5 *Fill the spaces between the flowers with smaller heads of bupleurum to complete the arrangement and to add a little more sparkly green.*

LILAC CIRCLET

 The foamy flowers of scented pure white lilac make an exquisite setting for a special dessert in late spring. Make a circlet of lilac with viburnum leaves to decorate the table, then bring in the dessert on a glass pedestal dish to stand in the centre.

MATERIALS
florist's foam ring, 20cm/8in in diameter
secateurs (pruners)
about 30 heads of white lilac
viburnum leaves

1 Thoroughly soak the foam ring and allow it to drain. Cut the lilac stems to within about 2.5cm/1in of the flowers and push into the ring.

3 Finally, add viburnum leaves to lend crisp contrast to the white of the lilac.

2 Position the larger flowers so they drape towards the outside of the ring and use smaller heads to cover the inside edge of the ring.

LEFT AND RIGHT: Sharp green and white always look fresh in spring.

MIDSUMMER'S PRIME

From bright'ning fields of ether fair disclosed,
Child of the Sun refulgent Summer comes.
JAMES THOMSON (1700–1748)

ABOVE: Fresh summer greens can be wonderful, understated and elegant. Here, a
single spiky artichoke head is offset by a jar of yarrow leaves.

LEFT: Roses are early summer's crowning glory, scrambling over
hedgerows all over the countryside.

The frontier between late spring and early summer is a blurred one. There is no first blossom to watch for, as in early spring, or symbols such as tulips and hyacinths, the flowers that epitomize the first warm days of the year. This seasonal transition is more subtle. By late spring, hedgerows and gardens are full of life, but gradually the flowers seem to change. The colours become softer, the petals more subtle, the greens deeper, replacing the fresh limey shades of earlier months. Then the rosebuds appear and we know summer is really on its way.

If there is an icon of summer, it is the rose. Most varieties will not flower until midsummer, but the wait is worth it. They're such eager shrubs, laden with sweetly scented blooms. Even those that produce just a single flush of flowers can provide such an abundance that there is plenty to cut and use. In fact, unless they produce pretty rosehips that you want to leave to develop for the autumn, it's a good idea to pick and deadhead, harvesting the last few blooms before the hips establish. That way, you may well be rewarded with a second show, though it will be less enthusiastic than the first.

Use roses for wreaths, garlands and candle rings; slip single flower heads into oyster shells as a pretty table decoration. Or gather scented petals as they fall, to use as an ingredient in summer pot-pourri. Early summer is the time when

LEFT: Red berries, cherries and delicate wild strawberries ripen in the early summer sun. Seasonal fruit such as this can be used as decoration and display as well as for eating. Buy or pick the fruit before it is fully ripe, pile it into your most attractive bowls lined with leaves and set on windowsills or dining room tables for a perfect scent and sight of summer.

ABOVE: Exquisite, scented roses are the glory of the garden at midsummer, and are perhaps the best-loved symbol of the season. If you have an abundance of the flowers and can pick at will, keep your arrangements simple with an abundance of the same blooms casually placed in an unfussy container. If your roses are less easily come by, choose a single stem — the most perfect you can find — and display it on its own in a tall, slender vase. This would make the perfect guest's room decoration, understated and elegant.

herbs are at their best, putting on enthusiastic
fresh new growth almost daily. Herbs really ben-
efit from cutting as, once they have been allowed
to flower, the leaves take second place and
diminish in size.

With their delicate flowers, herbs provide an
abundant source of wild-looking plant material from your own back yard. Use them to create
scented tablecentres, wreaths and garlands.

Early summer flowers are less succulent than
those of spring bulbs, and this brings a whole
new dimension to wildcrafts. Now is the time
to begin preserving leaves and flowers by pressing them. You can use them to make pictures
and decorate stationery, or incorporate them
into decoupage as a lasting souvenir of this
season of fresh, lush growth.

*RIGHT: Flamboyant poppies are wonderful to use
fresh, but do have a very limited life span once they are
picked. Retain the vibrant colour and delicate, papery
feel by pressing individual petals to preserve them.*

FLOWER AND HERBY NAPKIN RINGS

 What could be more charming than simple napkin rings made from fresh meadow herbs and flowers? Make these rings at the last minute and spray them with water to keep them fresh.

MATERIALS

FOR THE DAISY RING:

wire cutters

garden wire

florist's (stem-wrap) tape

daisies

scissors

plant spray

FOR THE HERB RING:

fennel flower head

scissors

green raffia

lavender flowers

plant spray

MAKING A DAISY RING

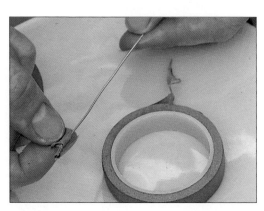

1 To make the daisy ring, cut a piece of garden wire long enough to encircle a napkin and bind the end with florist's (stem-wrap) tape. You might find it helpful to roll the napkin up and use it to measure the wire.

2 Wrap the tape around the wire, binding in flowers as you go to cover the wire completely. Bend into a ring and tape the ends together. Spritz well with water in a plant spray.

MAKING A HERB RING

1 To make the herb ring, cut the florets off the fennel head. Using the green raffia and leaving a short length free at the beginning, bind alternate lavender and fennel florets into a small garland.

2 When you are sure the garland is the right length, spritz it well with water from a plant spray, then place it around the rolled napkin and tie the two ends of the raffia together.

SCENTED CIRCLE FRUIT BOWL

A pretty and fragrant way to serve summer fruit is to make a herbal serving bowl. This one of mint, flat-leaved parsley and fennel flowers makes a sophisticated green frame for the fruit, but if you prefer something a little more showy you could add some daisies, such as feverfew, which would look charming. Herbs are inclined to wilt easily, so give them a good drink before you begin, and make up the circle at the last minute. You will need quite a lot of material to fill the ring, so the trick is to choose seasonal herbs, which will be abundant and give a lush, deliciously aromatic finished effect.

MATERIALS
florist's foam ring, 20cm/8in in diameter
scissors
large bunch of mint
large bunch of flat-leaved parsley
2 fennel flower heads
kitchen knife
plate to fit inside ring
plant spray

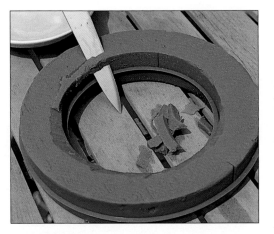

1 Soak the florist's foam ring until it is wet through. Snip off the ends of the herb stems and plunge them into water until you are ready. Shave off the inner edge of the foam ring to give a softer shape.

2 Set the plate in the ring. Cut the mint stems to about 15cm/6in and arrange all around the ring to create a base. Make sure the inside edge is well covered.

3 Prepare the flat-leaved parsley in the same way as the mint. Use to fill in any spaces, and generously fill the lower edge, making a "skirt" to cover the plastic base of the ring completely.

4 Cut off the fennel florets and use to add decoration. Spritz well with water before arranging fruit on the plate in the centre.

SUMMER POSIES

 The abundance of early summer flowers is irresistible. Each week, there's a new crop of fresh natural beauty that always manages to surprise, even though it was with us at exactly the same time last year. It is a joy to capture some of this beauty, putting flowers into simple containers such as jugs and jars to set off the beauty of the blooms without overwhelming them. There's no need to denude the garden or hedgerow at this time of year: take just a few of the flowers that are out in profusion – they'll look wonderful indoors, where you can appreciate their beauty close up.

BELOW: Even so-called weeds from the field can look delightful if they are cut and put into a vase at home. Be careful what you pick from the hedgerows, though: many varieties are protected, and anyway, few survive long after cutting. There is no problem with this cow parsley, however, which can be picked legally, grows in profusion in the summer and lasts well in water.

ABOVE: Love-in-a-mist, or nigella, is one of the prettiest annuals, and the plants are easy to grow.

BELOW: Simple arrangements can be very effective, try a single artichoke or a handful of ferns in a jar.

RIGHT: Roses always look romantic and it's no wonder that they have inspired poets for centuries. They are generous with their blooms and should be enjoyed indoors too. Older shrubs offer up armfuls of flowers without affecting the show in the garden.

SHELL BASKET

The smooth shiny surface of cowrie shells is a beautiful foil for the rugged texture of basketwork. A simple and inexpensive basket from the Far East can be given an exotic look with a pretty fringe of cowries, and used to store anything from onions and garlic in the kitchen to linens, handkerchiefs or even sewing theads. Alternatively, use it as a wonderful container for an unpretentious dried flower arrangement, or use it as somewhere to display the shells and pebbles you collected from the beach when you were last on holiday.

MATERIALS

needle

nylon thread

scissors

natural raffia

cowrie shells drilled at both ends

basket

glue gun and glue sticks

TIP
The shells need to have holes drilled with a fine bit before threading, unless you can find them with ready-made holes: these were cut from an inexpensive shell mat.

1 Thread a needle with nylon thread and knot the two ends together. Cut a piece of raffia about 5cm/2in long and bring the nylon thread around its centre, passing the needle back between the knotted threads. Pull tight so the raffia is now firmly held at the end of the thread. Pass the needle through the hole at one end of a cowrie shell.

2 Bring the needle up through the hole at the other end. Repeat with four more shells, to make a string of five.

3 Sew the shells firmly to the rim of the basket, taking the thread to the inside to secure it. Cut the thread and repeat the process until you have completed the fringing.

4 Using the glue gun, stick a border of single cowrie shells around the rim of the basket to complete the decoration. Make sure you have enough shells before you begin to do this, and plan how close they can be.

LEAF PICTURES

Leaves make charming pictures, and can be used to create endless different effects. They need to be pressed first, to thoroughly preserve them. There's no need to be too ambitious: show off the beauty of the leaves at their best by selecting pretty shapes and displaying them simply in a frame. Don't be tempted to use adhesives, which can be messy. Simply lay the leaves on the glass, add a backing sheet and re-assemble the frame.

ABOVE: Yarrow (achillea) leaves have a wonderful feathery quality, and they grow in profusion. Press lots of leaves so you have plenty of choice when making up the arrangement. These leaves have been mounted on a piece of Mexican bark paper, but any creamy textured paper background will do.

LEFT: Wisteria leaves look quite different when displayed in isolation. Make use of the graceful curves of their stems and mount them cropped close in a beechwood frame.

BELOW: If you can find or construct a frame with two pieces of glass, this can be a wonderful way to display prettily shaped leaves such as maple. Just choose one beautiful specimen and show it off in all its glory, so it appears to float in the frame.

RIGHT: Simple leaf pictures can look highly effective when grouped together. The key is to make uncluttered arrangements of the leaves, taking your inspiration from old botanical prints. That way, they complement rather than compete with each other.

WILD GARLAND

Wild-looking flowers make the prettiest table garlands for summer celebration meals. Garlands do use a lot of material, so it's better not to rely on the countryside. If you don't have enough suitable flowers in the garden, look in the florist for cultivated versions.

MATERIALS

FOR ABOUT 1M/3FT GARLAND

2 blocks florist's foam

kitchen knife

garland cradles or chicken wire (see Tip)

secateurs (pruners)

2 large bunches of dill

2 bunches of bupleurum

2 bunches of knapweed (Centaurea montana)

plant spray

TIP

If you can't get garland cradles, make the support for the garland from chicken wire. Cut a rectangle of chicken wire to the desired length of the finished garland and about 20cm/8in wide. Cut the foam into blocks about 5cm/2in wide and deep and lay these along the chicken wire, then roll up into a sausage.

1 Thoroughly soak the florist's foam in water, then cut it up into blocks to fit the garland cradles. Cut the dill stems to about 2.5cm/1in and position in the foam to create a base.

2 Cut off the individual heads of the bupleurum and add them all along the garland for texture.

3 Finally, decorate the garland with the knapweed heads for some added colour. Thoroughly spritz with water using a plant spray.

LEFT: Frothy white dill, green bupleurum and pretty purple knapweed (Centaurea montana) make a wonderful wild-looking garland.

ROSE CANDLE RING

A candle ring of garden roses, set in a footed bowl, makes a most delightful summer tablecentre. The roses don't have to be all the same variety – a mixture looks charming – so there is no need to denude one shrub. Adding in a few rosehips lends a little structure to the arrangement and gives a slightly wilder look.

MATERIALS
florist's foam ball
kitchen knife
footed glass bowl
candle
secateurs (pruners)
selection of garden roses, including hips

1 Thoroughly soak the florist's foam ball in water – this should take at least half an hour. Cut in half.

2 Place one of the soaked half-balls in the bowl and push the candle into the middle.

LEFT: Pick full-blown roses from the garden – the delicate yellow stamens in the centres add extra appeal.

3 Cut the rose stems to a length of about 2.5cm/1in. Arrange the roses to cover the foam base completely.

4 Add a few leaves and bunches of rosehips to complete the candle ring and give it a wilder, less contrived personality.

SUMMER POT-POURRI

 Capture the scent of summer by making your own pot-pourri. Lavender provides a wonderful aromatic base and retains its scent for many months. Roses can be another ingredient from the garden, supplemented if necessary with bought dried petals. The perfumes will then need to be enhanced by essential oils and fixed with orris root to make a glorious reminder of summer that will last right into the winter.

MATERIALS
6ml/120 drops lavender essential oil
5ml/100 drops geranium essential oil
small bottle
25g/1oz ground orris root
15g/½ oz whole cloves
15g/½ oz dried mace
115g/4oz dried lavender
225g/8oz dried rose petals
225g/8oz dried rosebuds
mixing bowl
wooden spoon

RIGHT: Deep purple lavender and delicate pink garden roses go together perfectly, and make a fragrant and pretty base for summer pot-pourri.

1 First make up a blend of the essential oils in a small bottle and shake well. Add a little of this to the ground orris root and stir to create a crumbly mixture.

2 Add the rest of the blended oil to the dried spices and mix well. Cover and leave in a dark place for 24 hours to allow the fragrances to mingle.

3 Gather together the dried petals and flowers, then mix them together in a large bowl using a wooden spoon. Add the dried spices, now well scented by the blended oils, and mix these in well. Add the orris root mixture, and stir well again. Cover and leave in a dark place for up to 6 weeks.

MEXICAN BARK FOLDER

 The subtle natural tones of Mexican bark paper, driftwood and raffia combine beautifully to make exquisite gift stationery. Fill this lovely folder with toning paper and envelopes to make a present that would delight anyone, of any age, for any occasion.

MATERIALS
paper and pencil for template
scissors
Mexican bark paper or other firm paper
natural raffia
small piece of driftwood
craft glue
darning needle

1 Copy the template from the back of the book, scale it up to a size to fit your stationery, and cut it out. Cut out the shape in Mexican bark paper. Cut four small squares from the remaining bark paper. Cut a length of raffia and wrap it around the driftwood, tying it firmly. Add a spot of glue underneath to secure. Mark the spot on the front of the folder where the driftwood toggle is to go. Thread the needle with a strand of raffia and pass the needle through one small paper square, then through the marked spot, from the back.

2 Thread a second small paper square on to the needle, then pass the needle through the raffia band on the driftwood and back again to the back. Knot the two ends of the raffia securely at the back and trim.

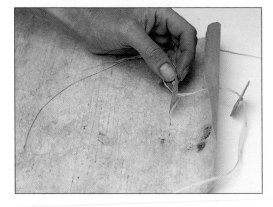

3 Mark the position for the raffia loop on the flap of the folder, aligning it with the toggle. Place the four paper squares in position, pass the needle from the back of the folder, then, leaving a loop, pass it back through the same hole.

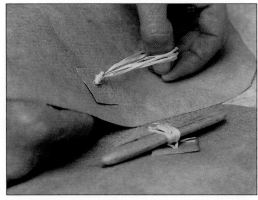

4 You will need to make a knot at the base of the loop. Gauge the position of this by trying the loop over the driftwood, allowing a little extra length for the knot. Make the knot, try the loop over the toggle again and adjust if necessary. At the back of the flap, tie another knot to secure the loop. Trim the ends of the raffia.

5 Turn in the side flaps and glue the front of the pocket in position. Leave to dry before filling the folder with some appropriate stationery.

SUMMER WREATH

 The unlikely combination of wild cow parsley and pale pink garden roses makes an incredibly pretty wreath. The frothy texture of the cow parsley makes an exquisite contrast with the creamy-smooth petals of the roses.

MATERIALS
florist's foam ring
garden and wild roses
large bunch of cow parsley
secateurs (pruners)

2 Continue to add roses until you are happy with the arrangement. Add rosebuds, rosehips and leaves if you want a wilder look. Fill in with the cow parsley for a pretty finished effect, covering the foam ring completely.

1 Immerse the florist's foam ring in water for up to half an hour, until thoroughly soaked. Gather together the plant material. Start by positioning the roses, first cutting the stems to about 2.5cm/1in.

3 Finally, add a few single or wild roses, taking care that they are not swamped by the other flowers. Give the wreath a good spritz with water.

HIGH SUMMER

Fair flowers that are not gather'd in their prime,
Rot and consume themselves in little time.

William Shakespeare (1564-1616)

ABOVE: *Shells from the beach make beautiful decorative peices all by themselves, and will also remind you of your summer holiday.*

LEFT: *Late summer flowers have mellower hues than early summer blooms, and many, like lavender, carry scented oils to protect them from drying out in the heat.*

99

The sheer variety of flowers and leaves in summer is astonishing. As the season progresses, it seems there is no end to new arrivals, and then, as the days get hotter, the countryside takes on a much drier look. Many late summer flowers have small, papery petals, and some almost dry on the stem. Think of lavender, yarrow, statice, thistles or alliums, those fabulous globe-like flowers produced by the onion family.

ABOVE: Gloriously architectural, artichoke heads look wonderful simply standing in a large glass jar.

LEFT: Place a single head of cow parsley in a small glass jug as an instant and pretty table decoration for a summer afternoon.

Late summer is one of the best times of the year to collect material that can be preserved: while in early summer you can begin to press plant material, late summer is the time of year to harvest and dry flowers and leaves that can be used immediately, or stored, ready for use during the longer autumn nights.

Dried material that you plan to keep should be stored carefully as it is very brittle. The best plan is to hang it upside down in a well-ventilated room where it won't be knocked. Alternatively, store it, well protected with plenty of paper tissue, in roomy boxes in a cool, dry place. That way it should last well into winter.

Hotter days take us outside: on trips to the beach and the river bank, both rich sources of material that can be used to make all manner of things. Even the smallest pieces of driftwood can be put to good use, and shells always have a place in the repertoire of wildcrafts. Give children a bucket each, and they will enjoy seeking out pretty pebbles and shells, as well as unusual pieces of driftwood.

If the call of the great outdoors precludes much in the way of creativity, use this as a time to build up a bank of material for future use when the nights draw in. However, there are some things, such as lavender and eucalyptus wreaths, that are best made while the material is still fresh and pliable. Once completed, they can be allowed to dry, providing decoration right through the winter.

RIGHT: Thistles and driftwood, shells and leaves are just a small part of the rich supply of materials offered by nature in the summer months.

OYSTER CANDLE RING

Oyster shells make the prettiest candleholders, and are easy to get hold of from most fishmongers. With a nightlight (tealight), scented if possible, in each one, they become charming low-level lights for the table. Here, several have been arranged in a circle with other shells filled with water to hold roses.

MATERIALS
12 oyster shells

6 nightlights (tealights)

scissors

6 roses

1 Arrange the oyster shells in a circle, some rugged side up. Place a nightlight (tealight) in six of the shells.

2 Fill some of the remaining shells with water. Cut the rose stems very short and arrange in the shells.

ABOVE: The rugged layered and fluted undersides of oyster shells make a fabulous contrast with the glossy, luxurious mother-of-pearl insides. Arrange the shells so that insides and outsides both show.

ABOVE: Oyster-shell candles make pretty table lights that are far below eye level, and so will never dazzle. Don't leave them burning unattended.

LEFT: Delicate pinky-cream rose petals look perfectly wonderful set against the rugged undersides of mature oyster shells.

THISTLE POT

Thistles dry easily and their textural quality makes for glorious everlasting arrangements. Late summer is the time to pick or buy thistles — look for those that have a dense, feathery appearance. Here *eryngium* (sea holly) has been used.

MATERIALS
2 blocks of florist's dry foam
kitchen knife and board
florist's reel wire
container about 15cm/6in wide
washing-up or garden gloves
about 100 heads of large thistles
secateurs (pruners)

2 Using the kitchen knife, cut off the bottom of the florist's foam so that it fits into the container. Check for size and trim if necessary.

4 Put on the washing-up gloves to protect your fingers. Cut the thistle stems to about 2.5cm/1in and begin by fixing in the bottom row.

1 Place the blocks of foam on the board side by side and wire them together using a piece of reel wire.

3 Trim off the top corners of the foam block to create an obelisk shape, then fit the block into the container.

5 Continue to fix in the thistles so that they cover the whole of the obelisk.

EUCALYPTUS WREATH

Eucalyptus is a fabulous foliage. Robust yet not rigid, it falls prettily and its wonderful bluey-green shades are most sympathetic to many colour schemes. There are many varieties: the young leaves may be round or oval, like those used here. The foliage of mature trees is much longer and more feathery. Once made, this wreath can be hung up and will dry naturally.

MATERIALS
garden wire
florist's (stem-wrap) tape
heavy gauge florist's reel wire
large bunch of eucalyptus

2 Using reel wire, attach a small branch of eucalyptus to the ring. Wire the other end of the stem to the ring. Add another branch of eucalyptus, again wiring it at the top and bottom.

1 Using three thicknesses of garden wire, make a circle about 36cm/14in in diameter and bind with florist's (stem-wrap) tape.

3 Add extra branches to fill out the wreath. Continue in this way all around the wire ring until the wreath is complete and looks rich and lush.

SHELL FISH WALL HANGING

This witty fishy wall hanging is deceptively easy to make, and the overall effect is reminiscent of a Victorian shell grotto. The trick when working with shells is to keep the design simple, and use them to suggest relevant textures. Here, the rhythmic arrangement of the mussel shells mimics scales, while small cowries are used for a finer-textured nose and spiral-shaped augers naturally fan out for the tail.

MATERIALS
paper for template

scissors

sheet of 1mm/³⁄₁₀₀in plywood, at least 50 x 18cm/20 x 7in (available from model shops)

soft pencil

fine jigsaw or heavy-duty craft knife

quick drying primer

paintbrush

grey-green emulsion (latex) paint

glue gun and glue sticks

small sundial shell or similar

small cowrie shells

mussel shells

5 augur shells

a few tiny shells

1 Enlarge the fish template from the back of the book to a length of about 50cm/20in. Cut out. Place the template on the plywood and draw around it and cut out the fish shape using a jigsaw or a heavy-duty craft knife. Brush on primer and allow to dry. Paint with a coat of grey-green emulsion (latex) and leave to dry.

2 Stick on the shells using a glue gun. Start by positioning the eye, then arrange the cowries for the nose and head.

3 Arrange the mussel shells in rows, sticking on the first row with the flat edge up; the next with the flat edge down. Where necessary, to retain the curved shape of the fish, you may have to turn some shells the other way at the edges. Try out each row to check that it fits before you start to glue it.

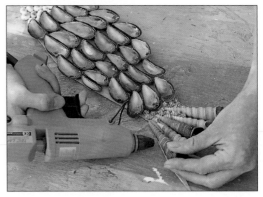

4 Arrange and glue the augurs for the tail, letting them fan out with the wide ends at the tail, then fill in with tiny shells around the points of the augurs.

QUICK WAYS WITH LAVENDER

 The heady, slightly medicinal aroma of lavender, redolent of summer, is hard to resist at any time of the year. It retains its inimitable fragrance even when dried, and can be used to scent rooms and linens deep into the winter. Lavender dries readily both on and off the stalk, and when cut bunches are dried, they retain their wonderfully sculptural shape, though the deep purple tones tend to soften. This makes lavender an ideal flower for dried arrangements and wreaths.

LEFT: The intense tones of lavender look even richer when teamed with similar tones. Here, lavender has simply been put into old-fashioned sugar bags that complement it perfectly.

BELOW: Freshly picked lavender looks glorious just put unceremoniously in the simplest of bowls.

LEFT: Open bowls of dried lavender tend to attract dust. Taking inspiration from traditional pomanders, which have holes through which the scent is released, here the lavender is put in an old sugar shaker.

RIGHT: Lavender bags can be the simplest of affairs. Here, dried flowers have been tied up in an old teacloth to use to freshen and scent the linen cupboard.

FEATHERY ORGANDIE CLOTH

The delightful spotty guinea fowl feathers perfectly complement the delicate organdie tablecloth. The feathers are easy to remove from their pockets for washing. Buy plenty of them so you can select at least 24 of a similar size.

MATERIALS
scissors
1.1m/1¼ yd white cotton organdie, 120cm/48in wide
needle
white sewing thread
white tulle, about 100 x 10cm/40 x 4in
pins
white stranded embroidery thread (floss)
24 guinea fowl feathers

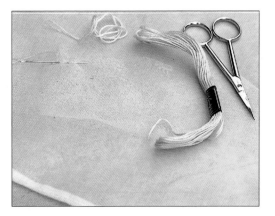

2 Cut the tulle into 12 rectangles, about 7.5 x 5cm/3 x 2in. Pin the pockets on to the cloth, arranging four in a diagonal line from corner to corner, then a parallel row of three on either side, and one near each of the remaining corners. With two strands of embroidery thread (floss), stitch each pocket into position, leaving one short side open.

4 For each corner, cut a strip about 22 x 2.5cm/ 9 x 1in from the remaining organdie. Fold each strip in half lengthways, turn in the sides and ends and slipstitch all around to make a tie. Make a bunch of three similar-sized feathers and stitch them to the middle of the tie. Tie the tie in a single knot around the bunch of feathers.

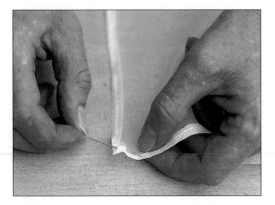

1 Trim the organdie to make a 110cm/43in square. Turn in and stitch a double hem around all four sides.

3 Select 12 similar-sized guinea fowl feathers, and slip one into each pocket, quill end first.

5 Neatly stitch a tied feather trim to each corner of the tablecloth.

HEART OF GOLD

Yarrow *(achillea)* is one of the most satisfying flowers to dry. It's an easy-to-grow perennial, and the glorious golden plate-like blooms begin to dry almost as soon as they open. Enjoy them in the garden for a few weeks, then cut them before they start to go brown. Strip off the leaves and hang them upside down in a dry, airy place, and in a week or so they'll be ready to use. These dense-headed blooms make wonderful dried flowers for providing solid colour, as on this charming golden heart.

MATERIALS
2 blocks of florist's dry foam
scissors
newspaper
pencil
kitchen knife
heavy gauge florist's reel wire
large bunch of yarrow
natural raffia

1 Lay the foam blocks side by side and cut a piece of newspaper to this dimension. Fold it in half and draw half a heart shape with the dip and the point at the fold. Cut out the template, unfold it and lay it on the foam, then cut around it using a kitchen knife.

2 Turn each heart shape on its side and cut in half so it is not so deep and bulky.

3 Use florist's reel wire to bind the two halves of the heart together. Cut the florets off the yarrow and push them into the foam until the top of the heart shape is completely covered.

4 Make a bundle of raffia thick enough to cover the side of the florist's foam base, fold it in half to find the middle and wind a piece of florist's reel wire around it. Twist the ends together. Push this wire into the top dip in the heart.

5 Take the raffia to the point of the heart and tie the ends together in a neat reef knot. Trim the ends. Finally, add extra florets of yarrow to cover any bare areas of the florist's foam base.

DRIFTWOOD MIRROR

The muted, weathered tones and contorted shapes of driftwood just beg to be used. Here, a shabby old mirror frame has been transformed using the curved edge of an old garden table for the top and various pieces of driftwood to make a wonderful organic decoration.

MATERIALS

driftwood of various sizes

old mirror in a wooden frame

screws

screwdriver

hammer

nails

2 Screw the main pieces of driftwood to the frame to ensure they are really secure.

1 Move the pieces around to create a design for the frame. If you need to widen a piece, simply screw on an extra section as here.

3 Add small decorative pieces of driftwood to the frame using a hammer and small nails, making an attractive design as you go.

LAVENDER CUSHION

 Lavender may be associated with a bygone age, but that does not mean it has to stay in the past. This cushion is up-to-date, yet still exudes that glorious fragrance. The inner sachet means you can wash the cover and replace the lavender.

MATERIALS
natural linen, 23 x 45cm/9 x 18in

matching sewing thread

sewing machine

blue linen, 23 x 45cm/9 x 18in

6 small metal buttons

6 snap fasteners

voile, 30 x 45cm/12 x 18in

130gm/4½oz dried lavender

1 Fold over and stitch a double hem along one long side of the natural linen. With right sides together, stitch the other long side to one long side of the blue linen.

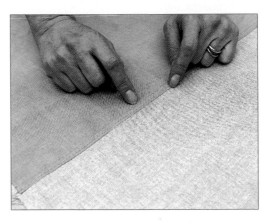

2 Press the seam allowance towards the blue linen, then sew a double row of topstitching on the blue side.

3 With right sides together, fold the whole piece in half and stitch the long side and the short blue side. Snip the corners and turn through.

4 Fold half of the natural linen section to the inside. Sew a double row of topstitching around three sides of the cover, leaving the natural side open. Stitch the buttons in place down the centre of the natural panel, stitching snap fasteners behind them to close the cover.

5 Make the inner sachet by folding the voile in half widthways and sewing around two sides to form a bag. Turn through, fill with lavender, fold in the edges of the last side and topstitch to close. Slip into the cover.

PANSY BOX

Pansies press extremely well as the flowers are flat to start with. They come in a vast range of vibrant colours, which will soften a little when dried, often to more mellow tones. Keep them away from sunlight to avoid further fading. This papier-mâché box has been decorated with pansies, then varnished for protection. It's a pretty idea that can be adapted to decorate all manner of things, from stationery and greetings cards to pieces of furniture.

MATERIALS
wallpaper paste
bowl
newspaper
plain box
gold tissue paper
patterned tissue paper
pressed pansies
acrylic spray varnish

1 Mix the wallpaper paste according to the instructions on the packet. Tear the newspaper into small rectangles. Dip a piece of newspaper into the paste, ensuring it is thoroughly soaked, and apply it to the box, smoothing out any bubbles. Continue until the box is covered with a layer of papier mâché. Allow to dry out thoroughly over 24 hours.

2 Tear the gold tissue paper into small pieces and apply in the same way as the newspaper to cover the box. Allow to dry.

3 Tear the patterned tissue paper into squares that are just a little larger than the size of the pressed pansies. Use the paste to stick a square of tissue to the centre of each face of the box.

4 Carefully dip each pansy into the paste and apply in the same way as the paper squares, making sure the petals are flat and uncreased. Allow to dry thoroughly.

5 Spray the box and the lid with a coat of acrylic varnish to protect the decoration. Keep the finished box away from bright sunlight as the pansies could eventually fade.

DRIFTWOOD COATHOOKS

 It is not difficult to find pieces of driftwood that have a hooked shape, and they can easily be turned into a wonderful set of coathooks, all for the price of a few screws.

MATERIALS
tape measure
long piece of driftwood or reclaimed wood
drill
small hook-shaped pieces of driftwood
2 pieces of driftwood, about 15cm/6in
long screws
screwdriver

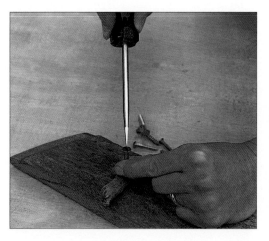

2 Drill corresponding holes in the bottom of each hook, and in the two mounting blocks. Drill some holes in the top of the mounting blocks for attaching to the wall. Screw the hooks firmly into position.

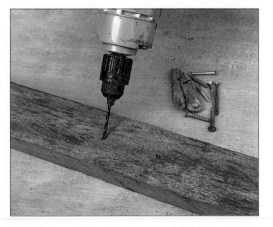

1 Measure the length of the long piece of driftwood and divide this by the number of hooked pieces to work out the spacing. Measure and mark the position of each hook. Drill using a bit compatible with the screws.

3 Screw the mounting blocks into position on the back of the main piece, near each end.

LAVENDER WREATH

 This glorious lavender wreath, bound with seagrass, makes an aromatic room decoration that will last all year. It needs to be made with lavender that is freshly picked and pliable.

MATERIALS
FOR A 45CM/18IN DIAMETER WREATH:

garden wire

wire cutters

medium-gauge florist's reel wire

about 250 stems of fresh lavender

green raffia

scissors

seagrass or similar thick string

2 Continue binding the bunches to the ring with wire. Pack them closely together to create a lush ring.

1 Make a 36cm/14in in diameter ring using three thicknesses of garden wire and bind with florist's reel wire. Make 30 bunches of six heads of lavender. Bind the first bunch of lavender on to the ring with wire.

3 Once bunches of lavender are wired on all around the ring, add more bunches but tie these into position using green raffia so that the wire is hidden. To finish, wind the seagrass string loosely around the wreath, and complete with a bow.

TEMPLATES

To enlarge the templates, use either a grid system or a photocopier. For the grid system, trace the template and draw a grid of evenly spaced squares over the tracing. To scale up, draw a larger grid on another piece of paper. Copy the outline on to the second grid by taking each square individually and drawing the relevant part of the outline in the larger square.

ABOVE: Decoupage Eggs

LEFT: Shell Fish Wall Hanging

ABOVE: Mexican Bark Folder

SUPPLIERS AND ACKNOWLEDGEMENTS

UK

THE STENCIL STORE
20/21 Heronsgate Road
Chorleywood
Herts WD3 5BN
Mail order available and stockists all around Britain of a wide variety of stencils plus brushes, paints and stencil sticks.

NORFOLK LAVENDER
Caley Mill
Heachham
King's Lynn
Norfolk PE31 7JE
Growers and suppliers of fresh and dried lavender bunches, loose dried lavender and lavender essential oil.

NEAL'S YARD REMEDIES
12 Chelsea Farmers' Market
Sydney Street
London SW3

Tel: 0171 498 1686 for other stores and stockists.
Essential oils, dried lavender, roses, rosebuds and other herbs, orris root.

VV ROULEAUX
10 Symons Street
London SW3
Tel: 0171 730 3125
Exquisite ribbons of all kinds.

SOMETHING SPECIAL
263–265 London Road
Mitcham
Surrey CR4 3NH
Tel: 0181 687 0128
Wholesale dried flower and florists' equipment supplier with a retail outlet at the above address.

USA

DODY LYNESS CO.
7336 Berry Hill Dr.
Palos Verdes Peninsula CA 90274
Tel: (310) 377-7040
Suppliers of pot-pourri, fragrance oils, dried blossoms, herbs, spices, dried and pressed flowers.

HERB SHOPPE
215 W. Main St.
Greenwood IN 46142
Tel: (317) 889-4395
Suppliers of bulk herbs, pot-pourri supplies, essential oils, herbs and others.

GAILANN'S FLORAL CATALOG
821 W. Atlantic St.
Branson MO 65616
Offers a full line of floral supplies and dried flowers.

TOM THUMB WORKSHOPS
PO Box 357
Mappsville VA 32407
Tel: (804) 824-3507
Suppliers of dried flowers, containers, ribbons, floral items, spices, herbs and essential oils.

AUSTRALIA

YUULONG LAVENDER ESTATE
Yendon Rd, Mt Egerton, Vic 3352
Tel: (053) 689 435
Fax: (053) 689 175
Lavender grower, plant sales (fresh and dried), lavender products (craft and cosmetic).

HEDGEROW FLOWERS
177 King William Road
Hyde Park
SA 5061
(08) 373 4499

ACKNOWLEDGEMENTS

My special thanks go to Debbie, whose glorious photographs have yet again made the subject sing; to Caroline Cilia, who designed the fabulous driftwood mirror and coathooks; to Deborah Schneebeli-Morrell for her exquisite decoupage eggs; to Joanne for her wit, encouragement and flair; and to Nigel for his elegant page design. And a very big thank you to my family, Richard, Zoë and Faye, for being so patient when the book encroached into the holidays.

Additional projects supplied by: Caroline Cilia, Driftwood Mirror and Driftwood Coathooks; and Deborah Schneebeli-Morrell, Decoupage Eggs.
Additional photographs supplied by Bruce Coleman Limited: p6,(t) by John Shaw, p6, (b) by Sir Jeremy Grayson, p7 by Christer Fredriksson.

INDEX